GOD IS A TREE

And other Middle Aged Prayers

D1601115

GOD IS A TREE

And other Middle Aged Prayers

ESTHER COHEN

God is a Tree and Other Middle-Age Prayers
ISBN 978-1-7364799-8-8
Library of Congress Control Number 2008930734

Design and Cover by Laura Tolkow

Pleasure Boat Studio books are available through:
Bookshop
Baker & Taylor
Ingram
Amazon.com
Barnes and Noble
Pleasureboatstudio.com

find me here

Overheardec.substack.com

esthercohen.com

*for everyone who's getting older
and for my mother who got there first*

If praying to God
did any good,
they'd hire people to do it.

Yiddish saying

It's not that I'm afraid to die.
I just don't want to be there
when it happens.

Woody Allen

ONE

I am
generally
prayerless
grown up
the usual Bas Mitzvah way.
More they
than we
Armenian anti-religious husband
secular Chilean son
world of Hindus, Hebrews,
ex-communists, union organizers,
poets, muslims, Cubans
I am the kind of person who loves
subways
have secretly started praying
not in the usual
sitting in a dark room way.
My prayers are unofficial.
They are anti-holy
They do not invoke
or evoke. I've never
liked the word blessed.

They are about Larry David and diabetes.
They're vulnerable, with no restrictions.
You can eat Krispy Kremes
While you're reading my prayers.
They're for my painter friend Marvin
who has Parkinsons now
and Chin at the Korean nail parlor
and Eddie Izzard
and you.

Amen

TWO

It's not
that I don't
have all those
what if thoughts
those same fantasies
only a little different
than in sixth grade
when Denny DiMauro
as dangerous as someone
could be at twelve
walked into Mr. Stamos's class
with his book disdainfully
balanced on his right hand.
Today so many
years later I can't count
today when I who
do not have a pilates body
have never jogged
even once
I who am even more imperfect
than ever

get into a Philadelphia
cab driven by a driver
with the amazing name of Palajifona
and he is even more beautiful
than Denny DiMauro
a man whose hands
hold onto the wheel
with a certain sureness
even now

Amen

THREE

Everyone
is younger
and thinner
than I am.
So what
So what
So what

Amen

FOUR

No one tells
Menopause truth.
You're incredibly hot.
You develop a small moustache.
It's hard to sleep.
Black cohosh doesn't work.
Your body gets wider.
Still, nothing big
truly changes.
At least there's that.

Amen

FIVE

Before I had
my hysterectomy,
I called eleven women
To ask for their advice.
Some said
never take out
your ovaries
I did. I have
never missed them.

Amen

SIX

On the train to DC
Sylvia said her one regret
was that she hadn't seen
more penises.
She raised this with eight women
traveling together to a political rally
They all more or less agreed.
Is it ever
too late?

Amen

SEVEN

I was sure I had
diabetes because
both my parents did.
Ditto grandmothers.
I went to the doctor
and asked him for a blood test
that can predict the future.
He likes blood tests, so he gave
them to me.
many. I don't have diabetes,
but I do have this and that.
My friend Marion wanted to
be comforting. She said
at least we're not on walkers .

Amen

EIGHT

Ira's Aunt Alice had been in a coma
for a while. She woke up
and only knew cleaning products.
That's all she remembered.
All she could discuss:
how to remove candlewax from
tableclothes, how to cope
with wine stains. The doctors
were stunned.
What could it mean
that her brain was gone
except for cleaning?
She went to visit Ira.
He bought her the book
How to Clean Everything.
And she did.

Amen

NINE

Today I'm finally
ready to write a prayer.
This is it.
I had a Bas Mitzvah
a long time ago.
I wrote a prayer then too.
God is a Tree was my title.
Louis Savitsky didn't like it.
Afterwards he asked me
why I had the chutzpah
to think that God was a tree.
His daughter became a Scientologist.
This is my prayer for you, God.
Tree or not.
It's more a song,

more Ry Cooder than Martin Buber.
I like them both.
You too,
on good days
when I can sit
under a tree
just sit.

Amen

TEN

When my mother
got older, her friend Selma
told her she looked fine
except she urgently needed
an eye job. She didn't do it.
It's my turn for the eye job now.
I don't like the idea.
But maybe.

Amen

ELEVEN

I'm often listening.
Sometimes I listen
too hard
too much
too often.
I'd like more white space.
I'd like more
time
Just to breathe.

Amen

TWELVE

Peter said
there are too many
film festivals.
Next thing you know,
he said,
there will be a
hot dog vendors film festival.
i thought it was
a good idea.

Amen

THIRTEEN

Today
I lost
my cell phone.
Again.

Amen

FOURTEEN

No prayers.
Not yet.
I want to write
a long prayer,
full of rage
and ritual, with jokes,
and moments
of unexpected brightness.
Moses may make
an appearance.
So will my mothr.
It will be an old poem,
located along the Mediterranean,
maybe in Ancient
Babylonia. It will be a prayer
with its own holidays.
Some will be familiar:
Passover
Ground Hog's Day.
It's late and I still
haven't written

my prayer.
Not yet.
Not yet.

Amen

FIFTEEN

Help me
not want more
all the time
to know I have
what I need.

Amen

SIXTEEN

Mitch turned fifty.
We went
to his party,
grilled radiccio,
wild salmon.
He told us
the title for the story
he might one day write:
Supplements
I have taken.

Amen

SEVENTEEN

Noah got
his driver's license this afternoon.
He said he was more nervous
getting his ears pierced.

He drove away.
I try not to think of
When he'll be back.

Amen

EIGHTEEN

Noah is from Chile.
When he took his SAT's
he checked Hispanic.
That was good,
better than Jewish, for instance.
He got many
university emails:
Dear Hispanic Student
We Want You.
I asked him
about his identity
and he said
he was intellectually Jewish
because of where he lives
but in a more serious way
he's a Buddhist.
Who knows about next year.

Amen

NINETEEN

In the middle of klezmer
and kugel, Anna Sorocer
emerged. Elegant large nosed
daughter of Label and Rivka,
she lived ahard life, gold earrings
notwithstanding. In the end, four
educated children later,
Beverly Hills apartment next door
to Rosemary Clooney's mother,
a block from Kim Novak,
she called her life a Big Success.

Amen

TWENTY

My teeth are a problem.
Every dentist makes me nervous,
especially those
who specialize in anxiety.
Dentist Pamela was a friend
until I told her words
are trapped in my teeth.
She referred me to a specialist.
We never saw one another again.

Amen

TWENTY ONE

Nina had an iffy mammogram.
Mark has a high PSA.
There's protein in Sheilah's blood.
Bruce's eyes might be getting worse.
Irv tore his rotator cuff.
Abigail has arthritis.
Judith has osteopoenia.
Oy vey seems
The only appropriate term.

Amen

TWENTY TWO

I didn't love her less
because my mother
was so difficult
but I wish she hadn't been.

Amen

TWENTY THREE

I'm still
trying
to get to that simple place
I don't yet know.

Amen

TWENTY FOUR

Who wouldn't want
to have sex with a lover
in the middle of any afternoon?

Is it better
to carry out as many
fantasies as possible,
or just to wish we could?

Amen

TWENTY FIVE

I've known forever
how important
secrets are. I've
had them since seventh grade.
Thank God for secrets.

Amen

TWENTY SIX

I've tried
to write a love prayer
for many years
but never could.
I have loved
all my life.
Who I loved
depended on the year
the moon
even music.
I'm glad
I've had
the chance to love
over and over again.

Amen

TWENTY SEVEN

The God I know
drinks vanilla milk shakes
and never abandons.
She is a very personal god.
She whispers
and is not afraid
to sing off key.

Amen

TWENTY EIGHT

It's raining. It's Yom Kippur.
Yoselle Rosenblatt sings Kol Nidre
on a CD in our living room.
Minda and Cliff eat chicken and tsimmes.
We don't discuss the holiday
but it's there.
Minda tells a sad story
of how her two dogs.
were taken away. Cliff describes
his childhood cat.
Noah is anti-holy.
He draws canoes.
Peter doesn't like holidays either.
I do, but I'm never sure
how to celebrate. I talk about
Bernie Goetz, who was interviewed
on the radio. He said OJ was guilty.
Peter suggested the press
ask Charles Manson and Jeffrey Dahmer
what they think of OJ.
We are all of us atoning.

Outside, the rain begins to flood.
Noah watches TVt in his room.
I listen to Yoselle Rosenblatt
over and over
and try to think of Jonah.

Amen

TWENTY NINE

The truth is I've had
a hard time with forgiveness.
Revenge is easier.
Last year I read four forgiveness books
talked to a few serious Christians and Jews
even a Buddhist a Hindu a Sikh and an
agnostic. I don't intuitively
turn the other cheek, and don't know how.
And I'm talking about pettiness,
not wars or larger wrongs.
I'd like to learn, and thought one way might
be
to say the word three times each day:
forgive
forgive
forgive

Amen

THIRTY

How many people
write Price Chopper prayers?
Probably not many,
given the huge number
of workers and customers
who pass through those
24 hour doors.
 I love supermarkets,
near infinite
selections of toothpaste, pastas,
sodas and soups. The way
we are all entitled
to watch brief one acts:
strangers choosing
cat food,
paper towels,
even frozen pizza.
Thank you for Price Chopper.

Amen

THIRTY ONE

I love the beach,
the chance to just lie there
without having to do a thing
especially laundry
just feel sun
on every piece
of my body
particularly places
long dormant
frozen from work
from snow, various anxieties
associated with middle age.
Mother husband son
work, the short story
of each day
and then in February
my son's school break
fortuitous middle class opportunity
to escape for six or seven days
to fly a few hours out and away
to sun and La Casa de Frances

spectacular hacienda
owned by irving Greenblatt
in Vieques, an island with problems
and beauty, wild horses, navy bases,
cows, unfettered, a bar
on the honor system, guests who don't play golf,
dogs and egrets
and a five minute walk
to Sunset Bay Beach
where no other swimmers
sit in a perfect white beach
soft and heavenly
sun enters my bones
at long last
at long last

Amen

THIRTY TWO

God is here today.
She is a spectacular god,
all good company
and magnificence.
She sings, barks
and is an able contortionist (she
learned this in India.)
She does splits
when you don't expect them.
She has a big vocabulary
is part Jewish
part Buddhist
part wind.
She plays excellent piano,
speaks Urdu,
breathes deeply,
and does the sun salute.
This god knows the words
to many songs.
She bakes bread,
and often bakes strawberry shortcake.

She turns these small mountains
so green you want
to eat them and then
she just hands you
a long light yellow porch
where you can sit
and sit and sit
to watch her move
so slowly
you'd miss her
if you weren't really watching

Amen

THIRTY THREE

I'm getting older.
I've never prayed before.
What I've done
On some occasions
Is mumble when the time
Seemed appropriate.
But now I pray.
It's hard getting older.
And it isn't.

Amen

THIRTY FOUR

We all need lovers.
Even now.

Amen

THIRTY FIVE

Slow it all down
a little.

Amen

THIRTY SIX

I'm more tired.
My eyes close
In movies. I can lie down
For a minute and disappear.
Dear God
Give me more strength
Without gyms
And jogging.

Amen

THIRTY SEVEN

I don't mind
If he has other women.
I do mind
That he takes us all
To the same restaurants.

Amen

THIRTY EIGHT

God
Of middle aged erotica
Welcoming hapless flesh
Sexiness of imperfection
Spider veins
Various saggings
Dear God of Eternal Erotic Desire
Abating only on occasion
Thank you for unending fantasy.

Amen

THIRTY NINE

God
Of middle aged sex
Give me more.

Amen

FORTY

Alarik's always
Wanted a wooden boat.
He's 65
And finally has one.

Amen

FORTY ONE

Another chance
Another time
Another day

Amen

FORTY TWO

Forget regret.

Amen

FORTY THREE

Harry's wife
Sara died
a year ago.
Harry's in Albany.
Public employee
with a beautiful smile
one tattoo per perfect bicep
Harry loved Sara.
He wants to love again.
Is that possible?

Amen

FORTY FOUR

I don't want anyone
To take care of me ever.

Amen

FORTY FIVE
Life change
Life changes
Life changest

Amen

FORTY SIX

Nina's moving
Aunt Lil's belongings
From her Queens apartment
to storage near a residential home
in Silver Spring.

Lory's going through her mother's
collection of Danish modern furniture.
Her mother will move in a month.

When my mother died
I gave everything away
Except for one small trunk..

I still want more egg beaters
for my collection.

Amen

FORTY SEVEN

Dear Metrosexual
Bisexual
Polysexual
Homo
Hetero
God
I never believed
For one minute
That you were celibate

Amen

FORTY EIGHT

Yiskador
Death impossible
and then it isn't.
Yiskador
You die
And other people
Friends and everyone
You love eats lox
And ruggelech
Talks about neighbors, kids
What life is
Eating lox
Rugglech talking about
What you can.

Amen

FORTY NINE

Sometimes I'm tired
not world weary
just tired
I want to come to a full stop

Amen

FIFTY

Keep me from talking about
Weather
Sickness
Children
Schools
Doctors
What I heard on NPR

Amen

FIFTY ONE

It's never too late.
It's never too late.
It's never too late.
It's never too late.

Amen

FIFTY TWO

I wish I could become
Buddhist
accept how life is
wish everybody well.
Too late
for that for me.

Amen

FIFTY THREE

I remember a time
When nothing hurt
When nothing hurt

Amen

FIFTY FOUR

Don't give up.

Amen

FIFTY FIVE

I could
remember every single thing.
Not anymore.
Names are especially difficult
who wrote who acted in
who sat next to me in seventh grade

Amen

FIFTY SIX

There's a lot
I'll never do.

Amen

FIFTY SEVEN

No matter
how old you are
you still keep looking
for God knows what

Amen

FIFTY EIGHT

Sue said
if today
was my last day
what would I do?
Certainly not dust.

Amen

FIFTY NINE

How can I
get you to listen ?

Amen

SIXTY

Here's what I don't want to pray for:
HDL
LDL
C-7 Vertebrae
Ulcers
Colitis
Leaky valves
Osteoporosis
Sore knees
Sore Hips
Sore shoulders

Amen

SIXTY ONE

Dani's
Back from
Ethiopia
with Shole, her two year old son.
In my lifetime,
families have changed.
Better now.
Not just blood.

Amen

SIXTY TWO

Some days
I write nothing
Just this
Just this

Amen

SIXTY THREE

What's with the personal ads?
Everyone says they want
To walk on the beach
Or go to movies.
Who doesn't?

Amen

SIXTY FOUR

Sue lives in Ithaca
Home of aging hippies
And songs like
Rosin your bow
Before you go.
She thinks that should be
Her theme song.

Amen

SIXTY FIVE

Thursday nights
I try to go to yoga.
When she says bend from the hips
Or breathe into the tops of your lungs
Or elongate your vertebrae
I still, after four years
Wonder what she's talking about.

Amen

SIXTY SIX

My favorite green silk dress
With painted leaves
Twenty six years old
Will never fit me again.

Amen

SIXTY SEVEN

Mel said the only positive
Of his mother's Alzheimers
Is he can tell her
The same joke
Every single day
And she laughs.

Amen

SIXTY EIGHT

Laura emailed
it's never
too late
I've always
half-believed
that was true.
I have to believe it now.

Amen

SIXTY NINE

Monday and I sit
On the porch
doing no more
than this:
words in a line
words on my desk
actually just
a red velvet chaise
no springs
facing corner skys
in eye sight
sky in earshot
sky in words
in a poem.

Amen

SEVENTY

If you don't
like it
try once more.
You'll like it better.
If not
Keep trying
Until
Until
Until

Amen

SEVENTY ONE

Nothing is slow.
Nothing is slow enough.
I was 35.
Now I'm not.
It was summer.
It's summer again.
My baby son
Is twenty two.
A car a job
A girlfriend.
I am not much different
from when I was a child
except for this body.

Amen

SEVENTY TWO

My Roumanian Bacau
to Beverly Hills grandmother
(she married Shmuel when she
Was 16, raised 4 children
In Grand Forks, North Dakota,
Lived for years
In walking distance of Kim Novak,
Ralph's supermarket
first ever Baskin Robbins
new flavor each day
she wrote each week to her 4 children
after she moved to LA.
The letters always began
with a modified weather report.
Sunny or pleasant, or
a little too warm. In LA
the weather didn't vary all that much.
She would end each letter
With the very same words:
take Care of One Another
Because Life is a Dream.

Amen